BOOK
WRITINGS
Volume II

~*~

~ Poems ~ Free Verse ~
~ Universal Themes ~

~*~

BOOK OF DIVERSE WRITINGS ~ Volume II
Poems ~ Free Verse ~ Universal Themes
Copyright 2015
By Mirta Oliva (a.k.a. M. Oliva)
Cover illustration and design by M. Oliva

CONTENTS

~POEMS AND FREE VERSES BY THEME~
~*~

PREFACE

|CHAPTER I – Love Poems (Pg. 1)

CHAPTER II – Motivational and Inspirational (Pg.13)

CONTENTS – [2]

|

(*) The Poem – Based on the Essay in Volume I.
   Excerpts of the Essay appear in the novel
   Sublime Adoption…
(**) The Poem – Based on the Essay in Volume I of
      Books of Diverse Writings

|

CHAPTER III – Abstract and Miscellaneous (Pg. 33)

|

|

CHAPTER IV – In Spanish (Pg. 37)

|

PREFACE

The standards for this diversified collection of poetry are best defined under My Poetry Styles – My Honest Disclaimer: *"I love writing... Poems or prose... But I must confess... Without apologies... My verses do not... Conform to the norm... Not Classic at all!"*

For the romantic ones, Chapter I has a great variety of Love Poems - some about eternal love and others not so lasting: *"As the churning waves loudly roar, I feel the Déjà vu of a love by me ignored..."*

Inspirational and Motivational poems in Chapter II include *"Don't let that big glittering star... Forever be your darkest cloud."* Some poetical versions include essays appearing in Vol. I of this series: *"There is no better feeling than feeling LOVED and WANTED - Two different concepts independent in their values but, when put together, they elevate the meaning of the word LOVE."*

Chapter III covers Abstracts and Miscellaneous poems - something to think about... *"Light in my shadow... Why did I question your game... When all the while you've been... A loyal guiding light... To keep me safe..."* The next chapter covers two Spanish translations of works from this *book* *"...Palabras al viento... Luna escondida... Entre estrellas perdidas... En el firmamento... Amour crescendo..."*

The next selection covers poems from published works, including Birdyjosh and Birdylu – A Paperbirds' Story in a poem. Chapter V includes six poems appearing in the novel Sublime Adoption – A Tale of Love and Mendacity. Excerpt from "I Am Not Your Judge on Earth:"

"I knew nada of my birth parents... Had no need to even search... That lack of knowledge, I'd say... Made them faceless... nothing beings... Inexistent they became... But something happened one day..." Chapter VI: Haiku poems.

CHAPTER I ~Love Poems~
~*~

|

1. FILL MY HEART WITH YOUR VERSES
~~Feeling the déjà vu of a past ignored~~

|

As the ocean waters
Each other embrace
And suddenly break away...
Our lives have moved apart
In obvious and cruel disdain.

|

As I watch the ocean sway
Forcibly moving back and forth
Pushing ahead huge crashing waves
In my despair... in some strange way
I am longing for yesterday.

|

As in the days not long ago
When you wrote me poems galore
Invoking a love that I deplored...
The tides have changed,
It is I who now implore.

|

As the churning waves loudly roar,
I feel the Déjà vu of a love by me ignored...
Repentant of my deeds I pray for mercy
Asking that you soon return
To fill my heart with your verses.

|

~*~

|

|
|

2. IN THE NEVERNESS OF TIME
~~(Yearning for his return…~~

|

Sometimes I ponder
What's on your mind...
Seemingly submerged
In the neverness of time.

|

But say nothing for now...
I can read it in your eyes
They tenderly speak to me
Without words… they tell no lies.

|

I feel the warmth of your thoughts,
How they subtly invade my soul.
They penetrate the core of my heart
They make me feel whole.

|

Be well, sweetheart, be gone…
Then, think of me alone
And when the time is right,
I know you'll be back, back in time…

|

~*~

|

3. KNIGHT AMONG KNIGHTS
~~End your crusade… vanish the wonder...~~

|

My gentle, loving knight,
You've been all over the world
Searching for amour sublime
With virile and endless might.

|

From towns to cities
At dusk or dawn
Under the rain
Or the bright, mighty sun.

|

Knight among knights,
You've met many ladies
Of honor, or maybe not…
For sure, you've seen them all.

|

My crusader of love,
You've now reached my abode
Having loved me like none before,
Knight among knights, travel no more.

|

With ardent kisses
You erased my candor
The pallor in my cheeks
And shyness in my eyes.

|

End your crusade here,
Vanish the wonder…
Be mine forever
My knight among knights...

|

~*~

|

|4. MY KIND OF MAN
~~So easy to love~~

|

It's been so easy to love you,
High in values, always true
Suave and gallant
Easy going, my kind of man.

|

With the passage of time,
We became two souls in one.
Raised two awesome children
I was yours, you were mine.

|

We are now aging together,
Not a bit has been lost
Of the sparks that once ignited
A love no one knew… but us.

|

~*~

|

5. MY OBSTINATE DESIRE
~~When you said that you loved me... ~~
|

When I first met you...
Remember that night?
You hardly spoke to anyone
Inscrutable... so quiet,
And I fancied your style.
|

When we met again,
My heart was pounding
You were enigmatic... reserved
Not much talk, just a cigarette
And I just observed...
|

When we met one more time,
You asked me to dance
We were close and yet apart...
How could I get to know
What lurked inside your mind?
|

When you came to me again,
You held me tight
And murmured things
I could hardly understand
Amidst our sweet romance.
|

We danced now and then
And during this quagmire
One day you said you loved me...
So in time you became
My obstinate desire.
|
~*~

6. NIGHT OF NIGHTS
~~Love message from the sea~~

|

Night of nights...
As the moon gleefully shines above,
Falling stars spray silvery rays
And a derelict wind blows across my face.
I then feel the warm embrace
Of this radiant night
While I wait for my love to arrive.

|

Night of nights...
Could that be him coming from afar?
I feel his presence ever so near...
But why is the wind swirling around me,
The shimmering stars disappearing,
And the moon beginning to hide,
As I long for my love to be here?

|

I prefer to ponder in vain
Than to hear the truth once again
That my love may never return...
But my doubts have now disappeared...
A guiding star brings his vessel so near
With flashing lights beaming in my eyes
Sending me a message of love so dear...
Nigh of nights, my love has arrived!

|

~*~

|

7. TELL ME WHEN...
~~Waiting for a long lost love~~

|

One day a few moons ago
You asked me to wait...
We were still very young
You wanted first and foremost
To explore the big, wide world.

|

So lo and behold
For years on end
I have wasted my days in vain
Sitting by the window
Hoping that you would return.

|

I've had many suitors,
Handsome, educated men
But I've always said,
"Not now... My love is on his way,
Come back some other day..."

|

But more days quickly passed
And not one letter had arrived.
I've been hiding the sorrow, I've buried the pain
That lurked in my heart without disdain
So my love, come now or tell me when...

|

~*~

|

8. THAT FURTIVE LOOK

~~The look that broke my heart~~
|
I was visiting a friend
When soon you came
You were shy, and so was I
Your eyes did not meet mine
A furtive look...
A word or two...
And then you left with a quick good-bye.
|
A long week passed
And once again
I visited my friend
Hoping you would return…
Later on you arrived,
Taciturn, somewhat withdrawn
That furtive look really broke my heart.
|
A week went by, plus another two,
And not a trace of you
So I called my friend who sadly said
"There is something you should know...
"He has a wife, he has gone home to her"
From that day on, I could never forget
That furtive look in your eyes...
|
~*~
|

9. THE DAY YOU SAID YOU LOVED ME...

~~It was too soon for a yes~~

|

The day you said you loved me
It was too soon for a yes
I was not in the mood as yet
My studies had to come first.

|

The day I fell for you,
My heart was beating for two
One million stars were shining above
And the moon was smiling at us.

|

The day you shyly proposed
I was happy just as you
Our hearts blended with love
With God's blessings from above.

|

The day we said good-bye
Neither one wanted to part
The moon was sad, very sad
And the stars lost their spark.

|

In time you asked about me
Too late to come to terms...
Our lives were apart too long,
I never saw you again...

|

~*~

|

10. WHAT NOW...? I ASK MYSELF
~~How to tell a man that the love is gone...)

|

When I think of a man,
Somehow... I think of you
When I think of love
It's that impalpable solitude
The longing that grows in my soul
And that's not you!

|

When you ask me
If I've loved you
You must already know
That my eyes can't convey
Even with deep inner sorrow
What my heart won't tell.

|

I then hesitate…
How could I just tell you
The sad truth that invades
My heart and my soul
With frustrating agony and inner pain
For this love that won't last another day?

|

But you want to believe my lies
That I love you with all my heart
When you have seen for yourself
In languishing and endless days
The emptiness in my eyes
So… what now? I ask myself...

|

~*~

|

11. WHEN YOU WERE MY WORLD

|

When you were my world,
You were my man and only one.
You could do no wrong,
You were my heart and my soul,
You made me feel strong.
    When I was your world,
    You wrote me poems of love
    For a reason… or none at all.
    You revered my name,
    And you spoke of me only, time and again.
Once a few years passed
We no longer shared that world
Strange forces took us apart
You did not seem to care…
And, apparently, neither did I...
    But one thing was not right;
    For all the years of shared love
    A sudden end without a word
    What could have gone so wrong,
    Wasn't our love worth a second try?
One day we saw each other,
We were silent for a while
Then a word after another
Made us fully realize
The meaning of years past.
    We have since bonded again,
    Living one day at a time.
    No promises have been made,
    Not yet… too soon anyway
    But our love is again sublime!

|

12. YOU ARE NOT IMPORTANT ANYMORE
~~Moving on with one's life...~~
|

We had planted a seed,
What we had is now gone
Our paths no longer cross,
I've moved to distant shores
You are not important anymore.
|

It was more like a dream,
It didn't make any sense
It was best for me to leave
It all came to an end
It was wise to let it be.
|

The times that we lived,
The promises we made,
The glory of my rebirth,
The planted new seeds,
The new paths on this earth.
|

No need to look back
No reminiscing of times past
No commitments remained
No point to return... nothing was left
No memories of what was then.
|

CHAPTER II
~*~ |
MOTIVATIONAL
AND INSPIRATIONAL POEMS
|

~*~

|

13. A STAR NAMED "D"
~In Loving Memory.
~To a good soul who left us too early~
|

A luminous star shines in the skies
She is not alone, but there she lies
Looking about and around...
Oh, how we rejoice to have just found
Her tiny twinkles pointing down
Forever watching her prior loving grounds.
|

Her name is "D"
No star beams so free
Yet, there she is for all to see...
With no regrets, forever at peace
She lived indeed a noble life
So full of glee.
|

~*~

|

14. AT THE END OF THE DAY
~~The value of honesty...~~

|

When all has been said and done,
Will I be proud of my rights or wrongs
Or feel my own scorn
From the life that's left behind...?

|

Was I fair and square
With those whose paths I crossed
Or did I steal the glory
Of those who deserved it most?

|

Was I honest… as honest as one can be
Or did I not follow my parents' rules?
Did I work hard, or just depended on others
For sustenance or most everything?

|

Did I lie to get my way, and caused misery or pain
Or was I loyal to family and friends
And helpful to those in need
To a small or great degree?

|

As we go over our conscience
Honesty should play first and foremost
'Cause there is Someone out there
Who knows... He knows the truth!

|

~*~

|

15. CHOOSING THE ROAD
~~Following the beaten path or the road less chosen~~
|

We can follow the beaten path
For an easy walk on smooth terrain,
Or take the road less explored
Full of roses embraced with thorns
Pesky pebbles and pointed stones
Making our journey on this earth
Difficult for us to traverse.
|

The choice should be the byway
That hardly a soul has surveyed
Full of holes, pebbles and boulders
Plus bushes with spiny clusters...
--But... what's there to be gained...?
The pride of not having derailed
From life's troublesome journeys.
|

~*~

|

16. DOG'S LOVE
~~A loyal and unique kind of love~~

|

Though I'm always busy
The job gets done
Friends come to visit
And so rings the phone.

|

But when the company is gone
And the calls come to an end
I am all alone
In my home, sweet home.

|

So God in His wisdom
Has sent me furry balls
Kind of crazy, kind of small,
Lovely bundles of joy...

|

To keep me company,
With loyalty and tender love
Perhaps as a reminder
That life goes on... with a caring dog.

|

~*~

|

17. EARLY IN THE MORNING
~~About family, friend or a loyal pet~~

|

I was to write a poem
Early at dawn
And my heart should dictate
All that could be said
This early in the morn.

|

And I waited for the message
My good heart should convey
That would drive me to say
In very short lines
All the greatness of this day.

|

But my heart refused to help
So I looked around and saw
Oliver, my precious beagle dog
Resting by my feet
And that was good enough…

|

"Look no further," I told myself,
"You know what makes a day great?
To know there is someone who cares
Be it someone you love
Family, friend... or your loyal pet!"

|

~*~

|

18. FOR THE LOVE OF ANIMALS
~~Kudos to animals for helping humankind... ~~
|

Why are animals on earth...?
There was long ago a change
From whence they came to be
To what we've made of them.
|

The once wild dogs now sit
On commands from their masters
They work for the handicapped
And also help in disasters.
|

The once unmountable horse
Serves man in many ways
They provide transport
And pull heavy carts with hay.
|

From a free flock of birds in the air
Now some live in ornate cages
To entertain all ages
With their singing and flying flair.
|

And what about other creatures
Big and small
That entertain us all
From the children to the adults?
|

Most people welcome their pets,
Who abide without complaints,
Always willing to entertain
Between chores and some rest.
~*~
Continued...

But there are more
Who take on so many chores
That help man in many ways
How could they be ignored?
|
In the interest of time
I shall end the list for now
But will surely be back
With zoo pets and many more.
|
~*~

|
Zoo pets,
Wild animals...
Valuable to us as well
There is too much to say
Of all critters of the world
Cared for and preserved in Zoos
Some in nice sanctuaries, or roaming free
For children and adults to pet or see
How they live, or how they act,
In cages or man made habitats
So I must close this verse
Praising the caregivers
For such special task.
|
~*~
|

19. I DO BELIEVE IN ME
~~Believing in oneself, in all that one can be~~

|

I do believe in me
In all that I can be
In all the good I may have done
In all the graces received
Not measured by silver or gold
But by things that matter most
Lending a hand to those in need
By deed or the written word.

|

I do believe in me
For walking difficult steps
To get to where I want to go
For not being idle
When there is so much to do
The list is big
I cannot stop or the wheel
Will forever rust and stop still.

|

~*~

|

20. IN THE IMMENSE OBLIVION OF TIME
~~Lives full of memories~~

|

Lives full of memories...
Some last, some fade away
Painful ones forever rest
In the immense oblivion of time.

|

With bad memories bygone,
Many good days are born
The sorrow has disappeared
Nothing to cry for... a new day is here.

|

The Glory of life has prevailed
All sadness in quick surrender
Let's open the Book of Happiness
With each page something's gained.

|

~*~

|

21. IN THE QUIETUDE OF DAWN
~~I am inspired… ~~

|

In the quietude of dawn
With the breeze caressing my hair
With paper and pen in hand
And with firm steady stand
Having not a single care
I begin writing these lines.

|

As my head dictates what to write
I find it warm and sublime
That my heart would take charge.
It rules… It commands!
Rushing me to improvise
A poem right from the start…

|

So I look up close and afar
For something to write about
And see myriads of flowers in bloom
Showing off their random hues
Plus chirping birds in rainbow colors
Swinging from one branch to the other.

|

I'm inspired... I can write so many poems
About flowers, and birds, and Koi ponds
The smell of tall grass dancing with the wind
And the vanishing moon sharing celestial space
With fading stars, and the shy rays of the rising sun
Yes, I can now start my poem in the quietude of dawn.

|

~*~

|

22. MEDITATION WITH LIMITATION
~~Meditate some; create more...~~

|

How much should we meditate
If we want to accomplish something?
Valuable time would go to waste
If we forever engaged
In a world of doing nothing.

|

So I want to stay inspired
To be creative, to finish what I start
Transcending into what I aspire
Seeking to light up
A millions sparks in my life.

|

~*~

|

23. MY PARENTS I FOLLOWED
~~ What was not to love about them? ~~
|
My father... always helping others
He was a rock of strength
He and mother taught us bout honor
What were we to do but follow?
|
My father, amiable and funny
My mother, kind of firm but noble
Their word was always honored,
We just listened and followed.
|
My parents were not perfect
But no man can claim that feat
They helped us in many ways
In ways we cannot repeat.
|
My father… the creative,
I learned his trait;
My mother, she loved her girls.
As a grandmother, she more than excelled
What was not to love about them?
|
~*~
|

24. OFF LIFE'S BEATEN PATH
~~ What's life without a little pain? ~~

|

I went off the beaten path
To live and learn
Through obstacles and pain
It was not easy then...
Stones were on my way.

|

Through droughts or heavy rains
I traveled rough terrains
Feeling not a slight disdain
It was a chore, I must say
But I learned my lesson well.

|

Twigs and branches left me scars
And some open wounds that still hurt
The work was hard, no time to rest
But I now feel all the wiser...
What's life without some pain?

|

~*~

|

25. OKLAHOMA ~ MAY 2013
~~After the vicious storm... ~~

|

Lives tormented by furious winds
Towns flattened by nature's ire
Blown away by evil tornadoes
Flora, fauna and pets suffered the wrath
Of the merciless, killer storms...

|

While most Oklahomans were spared
Some dear ones will forever be missed
But aside from rightful grief
Their spirits were not crushed
Oklahomans have remained strong!

|

~*~

|

26. REFLECTION AND JOY
~~ About Christmas... ~~

|

In the Holy days ahead
Amidst reflection and joy
We shan't revisit our past
Life pains we must forget
While praying from the heart
That the spirit of Christmas days
May forever last.

|

~*~

|

27. THAT LITTLE STAR

~~ A glittering star shall not be your darkest cloud ~~

If you happen to be that little star
Up above in the black, stellar skies
Don't try to pair yourself
With that larger, pointed light.

If you happen to be smaller in size,
Or different in your own right
You should fully realize
How much you shine inside.

Stand tall and be so proud
For you live a radiant life
Don't let that big glittering star
Forever be your darkest cloud...

Try if you will
And in time you'll see
What a big,
Bright star you'll be!

~*~

28. THE BEST YEARS OF OUR LIVES
~~What we had may now be gone… ~~

As the years
Push the months away,
Are we happier than we were yesterday?
Could we honestly tell the world
As we long for each day left behind
That we are just passing through
The best times of our lives?

I'll bet the answer is mixed
There is always something or someone missed
What we had may now be gone
But we must cling to our beliefs
Of a good life on earth
Despite sad memories of years past
Or a future unknown.

~*~

29. THERE IS NO BETTER FEELING
THAN FEELING WANTED (From the Essay)
~~Feeling loved and wanted by the ones we love~~
|

Years ago, I heard the comment
"There is no better feeling than feeling wanted"
Strong statement... I was impressed
And then I wondered what it meant.
|

With the passage of time,
It became mighty clear
The word *love* was quickly said
But the *want* was often spared.
|

Parents surely love their children;
They say love you much too often
But do *they all* spend enough time
To help and be with them always?
|

Some spouses claim the love
But their lives are usually afar
The want is not always there
They live a world apart.
|

Husbands and wives beware;
Parents, family or friends, please learn...
There is no better feeling in the world
Than feeling *loved and wanted* by the ones we love.
|

~*~
|

30. TRY IF YOU WILL
~~We must attempt to succeed… ~~

|

We all have something to give
We must attempt to succeed
And in the end, if we don't excel
Not all has gone to waste.

|

Having learned from it well
Failure thoughts we must expel
Only then we'll be fulfilled
So try if you will.

|

~*~

|

31. WHAT MAKES ME...

What makes me mellow?
Flowers in yellow
Weeping willows
Withering leaves
Moon in shadows
Stars sparkling
Sun in the hiding…

What makes me smile?
The moon so bright
Animals at large
Music playing
Dancers dancing
The skies so blue
Babies laughing.

What makes me think?
Any old thing
Drying lakes
Threatening skies
Rivers overflowing
Oceans pouring over the land
The world ever changing…

In the end, what makes my day?
A flower in red
Cute, loving pets
The fruits of the crops
Sunrise and sunsets
A sweet love story
And Nature in all its glory.
~*~

32. YEAR 1945
~~ World War II - The aftermath~~
|

Year 1945 around April and May
Important days to remember...
Enemy forces surrender
World War II had come to an end.
|

The world battling joy with pain;
History has shown that goodness prevails
The combined efforts were not in vain
A new era had started then...
|

~*~
|

33. YOUR ONE AND ONLY LIFE
~~ Be glad and enjoy the ride... ~~
~~ Adapted from the essay My One and Only Life ~~
|

You were given one life to live
For short or a long term
It is yours, do as you please
Observing the laws of the land
And giving someone a hand.
|

With no choices or preview
And no exchanges or return
Make the best of what you have
Be glad, enjoy the ride
It's your one and only life.
|

~*~

CHAPTER III
~*~

ABSTRACTS
AND MISCELLANEOUS THEMES
|

34. A CRUEL AWAKENING
~~ From betrayal and deceit ~~
|

I felt the betrayal
The spite and deceit
When I had given my best...
Though I saw it coming,
Denial set in
The treachery begot:
The cruelest...
And most rude awakening.
|

~*~ |

35. LEAVES OF ETERNITY
~~Swaying away like golden hairs... ~~
|

Oh, leaves of eternity
That gently floated in the air...
Now swaying away
Like golden hairs
Swept by the currents of time.
|

Oh, leaves of eternity
Don't abandon my precious grounds...
Come back to me
And forever stay by my side
To satisfy the yearnings of my life.

36. LIGHT IN MY SHADOW
~~Why follow me? ~~

|

Light in my shadow
Why follow me
Wherever I go
Day in and day out…
I try and I try
To escape your grasp
But I see you…
I see you
Just right behind
My body and my soul.

|

Light in my shadow
Why do you make me
To hide
In the darkness
As I turn on the corners
In all entryways
As I run to escape
Why do you follow
Every single day
My body and my soul?

|

Light in my shadow…
Why did I question your game?
When all the while you've been
My guardian angel,
A loyal guiding light
Who made me watch
Each step I was to take
To keep me safe
Trough life's upheavals
And the forces of evil

37.MUDDY POND OF AFFRONTS
~~Fight for What is Right~~

|

How much more can you take
Before your words explode
In ways that set you free
From a muddy pond
Full of hurtful affronts?

|

Be strong and be yourself
Don't follow the easy road
It's easier to give up
Fight for what is right and in the end
Let the mud end up on them.

|

~*~

|

38. PLEASE DON'T CALL ME FRIEND
~~We just met yesterday… ~~

|

Please don't call me friend
We just met yesterday…
Give us some time to acquaint ourselves
But even then...

|

Please don't call me friend
Not yet, anyway
There is so much you need to know 'bout me
And I must get to know you well.

|

Please don't call me friend.
So many years have passed since when
We've shared stories of love and pain
But I still don't know you well.

|

Perhaps the day will come
When I'll understand your inner soul
Though it may be near... for now
Please don't call me friend.

|

~*~

CHAPTER IV
|
~*~

|
POEMS IN SPANISH
|
39. MI PRIMER AMOR
~~From Sublime Adoption…
~~"My Very First Love"
|
Primer amor...
Profusion de sentimientos
Puros, inolvidables.
Noches sombrias
Palabras al viento
Luna escondida
Entre estrellas perdidas
En el firmamento
Amour crescendo...
|
En la playa desolada
Mis dedos amorosos
Dibujan corazones en la arena
Sellando nuestros nombres
Con una flecha robada
De Cupido, Dios del deseo…
Para anunciar al mundo entero
Nuestro gran amor
Eterno y verdadero.
|
~*~
|

40. REGRESA A MI CON TUS VERSOS
~~From the poem Fill My Heart With Your Verses~~

|

Como en los grandiosos mares…
Unas olas incansables se baten
Con fuerza extrana
En el fondo de mi alma.

|

Como las aguas que se enredan
En el fondo de un mar profundo
Con mi mente atormentada
Pienso en el ayer - nuestro otro mundo.

|

Como en aquellos lejanos dias
Que me colmabas de poesias
Prometiendo amor eterno
Algo tarde te contesto que te quiero.

|

Como las olas que rompen contra la arena…
Con ese mismo empeno, arrepentida,
Te ruego: Unamos de nuevo nuestras vidas…
Regresa a mi con tus versos!

|

~*~

|

CHAPTER V

|

~*~

|

POEMS FROM PUBLISHED WORKS

|

FROM: BIRDYJOSH and BIRDYLU-
A Paper Birds' Story
~*~

41. BIRDYJOSH AND BIRDYLU…
~~ (The book condensed In a Poem)

|

I managed the paper
With creases and folds
And soon you were born
My sweet bird of love
BIRDYLU was your name
And you flew and you played
Your eyes always calling
For a handsome paper mate.

|

So I went right along
And folded paper again
Then you were born,
BIRDYJOSH was your name…
The pair was in love,
I noticed one day
So I prepared a wedding
For the good paper birds.

|

Continued…
~*~

|

My prayers were answered,
You flew inside the room
Staring through the window
At the green leaves and blooms…
I only knew then
They'd be leaving my den
But I'd always be watching
Both birdies and hatchlings.
|

To get seeds and other goodies
They'd get out of the roost
Safeguarding their 'lil bodies
From the light of the high moon…
The birds built their nests
The chicks came and went
And Boxer my cat
Would not go near them.
|

For it happened one day,
BIRDYLU was surprised
A feathered-chick had arrived
It really blew her away!
With only one worm
What was she to do…
When two little beaks
Were begging for food!
|

Continued…
~*~
|

It was then that I told her,
You must feed both birds,
The one with the feathers
And the one of *papier*…
So BIRDYLU fed both chicks
And soon they would play
Minding not a bit
Of what they were made.

|

And when the time was near
For the feathered little chick
To join her own breed,
I saw more than one tear...
The birds shared the forest
Very close to my backyard
They all saw each other
By the silver moon at night.

|

One day I arranged
A big party in the skies
What a sight, what a night,
I could not believe my eyes!
With the colors of the rainbow
More chicks were born
They all lived in harmony,
They all shared the fun.

|

And BIRDYJOSH and BIRDYLU,
Dressed in red, green and blue
Remained always together,
Forever true…

|

~*~

|

FROM: SUBLIME ADOPTION-
~~A Tale of Love and Mendacity

|

42. I AM NOT THEIR JUDGE ON EARTH
~~My perception has now changed... ~~

|

I learned I was adopted
When I became an adult...
With my parents now gone
Should I then begin the search
Every night and every day
Of those who gave me away
Soon after I was born?

|

I knew nada of my birth parents,
Had no need to even search
Where they lived or if they'd died
Or who were they...
That lack of knowledge, I'd say
Made them faceless... nothing beings,
Inexistent they became.

|

Less than little to me they meant
Even my thoughts avoided them
But something happened one day
Someone dear called my name
"Are you okay, James?
"I have something good to say..."
--"Say whatever" –said I – "for my own sake!"

|

Continued...
~*~

"Are you sure you want to hear?"
--"What else can I say, Kate, go ahead!"
"James, your birth parents are alive;
"You know your birth mother by name
"But they both love you well...
"Their past behavior? Hard to explain!
"Want to meet them now, or when...?"
|

--"Kate, I have no choice...
--"If you think so highly about them..."
"Your birth mother... with us at the beach..."
--Yes, of course, I remember her well...
--"My perception has now changed
--"She now has a face
--"And I even seem to like her!"
|

"My question, again, James,
"Do you ever want to meet them?
"They await for your reply
"To repent from old mendacious ways..."
--"Yes, good friend! In the past, I shall not dwell;
--"Say no more, I'd like to see them, now or then...
--"I am not their judge on earth!"
|

~*~

|

43. MAKE AMENDS
~~ If you ever lied…It's time to make amends ~~

|

If you ever lied
About family or friends
If you told that lie time and again
But you never told the truth
To the people you had lied to…
It is time to make amends.

|

If you've hurt
Family or friends
And you saw the agony in them
How their lives forever changed
But you chose to ignore their pain…
It is time to make amends.

|

Whether you tend to
Shower your graces on others
Or to pray to God for redemption
Because "you are good…" Just do the math!
Don't ignore your painful wrath
Wake up my friend… and make amends!

|

Uncover the lies, relieve the hurt
Be brave before it's too late
Tell the truth… let it be!
Make amends!
And you'll be
Forever Free!

|

~*~

|

44. MY MOM IS NOT MY MOTHER
~~Dedicated to Kate and Bryant ~~

|

"What's the relevance...?"
I used to ask myself
"Of having a mom, but not a mother
"Of being loved by a man who is not my father
And be revered by a brother who is not my brother?"

|

From child to adult
I had never felt the void...
Only when I was told
It seemed to hurt to know
I was not who I thought I was.

|

I don't know who was the saddest,
My darling mom or my loving daddy
As they told their only daughter
In their sweet usual manner
They were not her birth mother and father.

|

If I had always felt the love
Of my sweet mom and dad
Why did it hurt to know
I had been given away
On the day when I was born?

|

I may have been adopted
My birth parents not always near
But I shall always bless each day of the year
I've been able to spend
With a mom and dad so dear.

|

Continued...

|
It no longer seems to matter
My eyes hold no more tears
I've forgiven my birth parents
At times afar, but yet so near
Their reasons are finally clear…
|
My birth parents,
I hold you dear;
Kate and Bryant, you've been the best!
I love you all, this is my quest:
My new life I shall revere… For I am here!
|
~*~
|

45. MY VERY FIRST LOVE
~~Dedicated to Frederic~~

|

My first love...
Stormy feelings
Palpitate in my heart
Pure, unforgettable
Forever to last.

|

In a somber night
Alone at the beach
I throw
Loving words to the wind
And draw
In the moist, cool sand
Your name and mine
Inside a big, pierced heart...

For the world to see
How we were meant to be
From the very start.
Our love shall forever last...
Nothing can take us apart!

|

~*~

|

46. PARADISE ON THE HILLS
~~About North Carolinians' hospitality…
~~And the area's beautiful hummingbirds
|

In the Old North State,
Somewhere,
The hummingbirds filled the air
Hovering around with a buzzing sound
As they flew up and around.
|

Colored in green, red and silvery blues
A rainbow splash
In their glaring suits
To show their beauty with vibrant flair
To the grateful guests of Joe and Claire.
|

The radiant hummers loved to flutter
Where the sweet nectar lies
Swarming the feeders by sunrise
Up in the air, how they glitter
So full of luster, so oddly still….
|

Oh, why those enchanting days
Had to end so quick
As we drove away
From the colorful and tranquil
Paradise on the Hills.
|

~*~

|

47. SHADOWS OF MY PAST
~~Life can still be agog… ~~

|

The present is here,
Real love and no tears
The past is just that
Old memories won't last
Though he is no longer near
I have nothing to fear…

|

The feelings are gone
We never belonged
It wasn't for real
My heart was not touched!
Life can still be agog
Despite the shadows of my past.

|

~*~

|

ABOUT HAIKU
(Introduction to Chapter VI)

I am new at this writing mode so I do not know all there is about these short and typically sweet messages. There are too many varieties of Haiku poetry and, for the reader who fancies them, there may not be a need to describe its format; conversely, for the ones new to these special poems, any information I may provide may not cover all there is to know.

There are great articles on the internet explaining the differences about traditional Japanese Haiku vs. the American Haiku, its format or theme preferences. There are Haiku writing groups and contests around the world that present the opportunity for interested writers to learn or improve their skills on the subject.

The beauty of Haiku is that the theme is usually a free, spontaneous style without any particular rhyme considerations. On the other hand, it is in some way a grammar and mental exercise.

In this last chapter, I have included a limited amount of my own Haiku renditions – my humble contribution to this fine expressive art.

~*~

CHAPTER VI - HAIKU Poems
|

48. A HAIKU VARIETY
~Inspirational Haikus~
|

Red flowers blooming
The rain rushing its downpour
Clouds dry; then relax.
|

Fresh air for my soul
My mind in the depths of time
The cool summer winds.
|

On the hills we rest
Lives in blissful oblivion
Deep meditation.
|

What's bout adoption
That makes it very sublime?
Love of humankind!
|

~*~
|

49. HAIKU "5-7-5" TO KATZ
~~To a beautiful gray cat~~

|

They could be kittens
Or bigger cats of mixed breeds
Surely so pretty!

|

At a gray cat's house
When least expected by all
Cat got on my lap.

|

She first looked me up
Took notice: papers on lap!
Then, the sudden jolt.

|

But soon she came down
To search my handbag
And guess what she found...

|

Make-up, pencils, pens
What a find, she thought, let's play
With goodies in purse.

|

Labeled arrogant
They just like to flirt and flaunt
Love cats, love them all!

|

I have owned two dogs
Beagle and Pom I've loved...
But Kats never owned me!

|

~*~

|

50. THE MANY FACES OF HAIKU
~~Haiku defined not in special format~~

|

In old Haiku we've seen
All the three lines of it
Five, seven and five
Or longer
If we so wish...

|

Words with one or more syllables
It does not need to rhyme
Variations there are
It's Haiku, you see
All the three lines of it.

|

Different they can be:
Do only fives!
Repeat the sevens!
With single syllables!
Do Haiku forever!

|

~*~

|

51. HAIKU TIDBITS

|

~~COUNTING HAIKU SYLLABLES

|

One, two, three, five, eight
I forgot six and seven
Too bad, too bad, right?

|

~~SINGLE SYLLABLE HAIKU

|

The bright moon looked down
It was the first of those days
When our round friend smiled.

|

~~SINGLE/MULTIPLE SYLLABLE HAIKU

|

The beau*ti*ful moon
Is look*ing at our good land
Wink*ing her big eyes.

|

~~HAIKU CHALLENGE CONTEST
~~My Submission to The Miami Herald

|

"The Haiku Challenge
What a Chance for Those Who Dream
Of Writing in Verse."

|

THE END

|

MY POETRY STYLES
(My honest disclaimer)
~ Poems~Free Verse ~
~ Universal Themes ~
~*~

I love writing
Poems or prose
But I must confess
Without apologies
My verses do not
Conform to norm:
Not Classic at all!
|

Of irregular length
With little or no rhyme
Punctuation at will
In open form - or mixed, why not?
They call it "The new free verse"
Never in meter
… It matters not!
|

With themes too many:
About fleeting or eternal love
Inspiring, Motivational, Philosophical
Poetical versions of Essays
Abstract, Haikus, in Spanish
Find them right here, in Volume II
Of Book of Diverse Writings.
|

~*~

|

WHY I DO WHAT I DO...
|

~*~

I...
Love humankind and animals as they deserve.
Write varied prose because I love to.
Create poems capriciously in many forms.
Paint because it brightens my day.
Sculpt once in a distant blue moon.
Believe in creation vs. vicious destruction.
Direct most writing endeavors to impart good-will.
Live to enjoy it all!
|

~*~
|

ABOUT THE AUTHOR
~o~

Once a writer, always a writer!

As a child, Oliva had a passion for painting and writing about anything that came to mind. As she matured, her writings were focused on anecdotes, essays, short stories and poems. Her most recent endeavors include creating fictional stories, sometimes adding a bit of dry humor and drama.

Oliva's paintings started with drawing the human figure in black and white after taking drawing courses in MDCC. Gradually, she delved in pastel and oil portraits, followed by oil renditions of landscapes and animals.

When it became necessary to divert her full attention to a successful career path in banking, she had to put aside all her artistic dreams. Down the road, after selective antiques collecting and planning, she opened and operated an antiques and collectibles store for a few years – appropriately named Antiques Are Forever, now inactive.

Dealing extensively with antiques and art brought her back to painting. Oliva's new emphasis was to study the masters' techniques by visiting museums or from already acquired antique oil paintings. A new artistic vision included abstracts and modernism.

At some point, the artist began writing and illustrating her works – a children's book and a novel. Later on, her collection included essays and short stories. Aside from currently published works, Oliva has others in various stages of completion.

For the artist at heart, the calling never ends...

~*~

WEBSITES

~O~

|
~~ http://www.AntiquesArtBookworld.com
Main Website and Blog of M. Oliva.
~~ The website focuses on her books and miscellaneous writings, including poems. Some of her art is included for decoration.
|
~~ The Blog: "Mirta's Blog of Pet Peeves, Ideas & Everything Else" is under construction.
|
~~ http://www.olivaarteshow.com.
This colorful Website is mainly dedicated to displaying her artwork – from realistic to abstract to comic divided in two sections.

~O~

CONTACT: SOCIAL SITES

~~ Mirta Oliva (artist-writer) ~~
LinkedIn, Facebook, Pinterest, Wordpress and others.
|
~*~
|

PUBLISHED WORKS

~O~

I.- BIRDYJOSH AND BIRDYLU ~ A Paper Birds' Story – A children's book fully illustrated in color.

An endearing story about a family of Origami-style paper birds and their struggles to survive amidst an unknown environment. The unusual, enlivened, birds have been depicted in several colorful, full-page prints from oil paintings, aquarelles and black and white drawings, created especially for this presentation. The artwork follows the chicks' path through a beautiful, guarded existence. Below is an excerpt from a party in the skies:

"… How happy we were to see that colorful array of paper birds way up in the air, feeding a bunch of baby birds. What a sight, what a night, I could not believe my eyes!"

~~O~~

Continued…
~*~

Published Works [2]

II.- SUBLIME ADOPTION ~ A Tale of Love and Mendacity. A novel for young adults and adults. Below is an excerpt of the SPECIAL DEDICATION:

This labor of love is dedicated to all natural and adoptive parents of the world and to all adopted children of any ages. The story does not lead to a merciless condemnation of certain characters for mistakes or actions in their past, but rather it focuses on the cumulative ill effects of lies and deception as the only way to deal with difficult situations. In the end, repentance and the power of forgiveness prevailed.

Other relevant parts of the story may promote and help to achieve a sense of acceptance and pride by those *chosen* children.

In most instances, birth parents do love the born or yet to be born creatures, but for some valid reason, cannot keep them. In the majority of the cases, the adopted children feel *loved and wanted* by their adoptive parents who *chose* to have them in their lives. Consequently, most adoptees do not feel rejected or abandoned; on the contrary, they tend to joyfully embrace the fact that one or two souls elected to have their hearts broken so that their natural child could enjoy a better life.

~*~

Continued…

~*~

Published Works [3]

|

THE GIANT TALES Anthologies

|

Three of this author's short stories appeared in two of several anthologies published by Heather M. Schuldt – a compilation of the works of several authors. Each story adhered to a theme and three highlights. All of these Giant Tales anthologies can be found in Amazon.

|

A.- From GIANT TALES ~ World Of Pirates,

|

III. "THIEVES OF THE SEAS" by Mirta Oliva

||

The above is one of the 53 stories from different writers who contributed to the World of Pirates anthology. The Thieves of the Seas story begins with what would be a wonderful and purposeful voyage:

|

"Baron Lockhart Lyonstaff of Southshire was leaving London with his secretary, Marianne. They were special guests aboard a big ship headed for the Caribbean where the Baron planned to finish his book, My Encounter with the Thieves of the Seas…"

|

Continued…

~*~

|

Published Works [4]

|

B.-From GIANT TALES ~ Dangerous Days (Anthology published by Heather M. Schuldt)

|

IV. THE GREEN INVISIBLE MOUNTAIN By Mirta Oliva

|

"Edward and Lilly were sitting on the swing in their L-shaped front porch overlooking the most picturesque mountain chain they had ever seen. Alongside Mount Green, the tallest one of the group, ran the sparkling Stony Creek. They considered themselves lucky to own this farm even though they were hours away from family and neighbors..."

|

V. IN PURSUIT OF A DWARF PLANET By Mirta Oliva

|

"A few months passed and only Mary was selected to join and manage the first taxi mission. Johnny was happy for her since, after all, his wife was the one who had found the planet and was more interested..."

|

~*~

|

Continued...

~*~

|

Published Works [5]

|

VI. BOOK OF DIVERSE WRITINGS – Volume I – Featuring HIDDEN – A Crime Mystery - [Prose Version].

|

Initially, all short stories and poems written by the author were to be combined in one volume. As the compilation progressed, it was decided to divide prose and verse in two separate editions. Volume I has already been published in digital and paperback formats.

|

Aside from the featured longer story in Chapter One, there are fifteen short stories with varied themes including action, adventure, family, fantasy, light romance, and Sci-Fi with two or three UFO encounters. Two anecdotes are followed by essays of honor, inspirational, motivational, philosophical nature, and some trivia.

Here is a peek at segments of Volume I:

|

a.- HIDDEN, A Crime Mystery – *Featured story*.

|

"… In a conscientious effort to take a different path to get home, Drew turned to the right following a seldom traveled dirt road leading to an old water well. As he walked, his eyes kept gazing down at the footpath driven by a commanding force. He must have been trying to avoid stomping on an impertinent stone when, suddenly, something caught his eye…"

|

Continued…

~*~

|

Published Works [6]

|

From BOOK OF DIVERSE WRITINGS – Volume I

|

Other Short Stories:

|

b.- THE DRONE, THE CABIN, AND THE SPIES WITHIN

|

"… When they got to the door, the couple noticed that it was unlocked. "How strange," said Hendrick. "I am sure that I locked the house before leaving. As they entered, they saw a note on the kitchen counter…"

|

Essays:

|

c.- WHO SHOULD DICTATE: MY HEART OR MY MIND?

|

"…While it is not easy to discern between the mind and heart's directives, I will try to delve into my encounters with mind reasoning and heart's impulses – plus my rationale as to which to trust…"

|

~*~

|

MAIN WORKS IN PROGRESS

~O~

A.- JOSELIYO Y LORILU – Mis Dos Pajaritos de Papel

The Spanish version of BIRDYJOSH AND BIRDYLU – A Paperbirds' Story (Translation completed; pending formatting and revision).

B. A Drawings Book – About one hundred drawings, all finished. (The narrative is being edited).

C. A series of about one hundred animal oil paintings suitable for illustrating children's books.